Learning
to Get
Along®

When I Feel Afraid

Cheri J. Meiners, M.Ed.

Illustrated by Meredith Johnson

free spirit
PUBLISHING®

Text copyright © 2003 by Cheri J. Meiners, M.Ed.
Illustrations copyright © 2003 by Free Spirit Publishing Inc.

Library of Congress Cataloging-in-Publication Data
Meiners, Cheri J., 1957–
    When I feel afraid / Cheri J. Meiners ; illustrations by Meredith Johnson.
      p. cm.—(Learning to get along)
    Summary: Explains that many things can be frightening and provides examples of different things one can do to feel less afraid, such as asking for help from a person one trusts. Includes information and extension activities for parents or teachers.
      ISBN 1-57542-138-0
      1. Fear in children—Juvenile literature. [1. Fear. 2. Conduct of life.] I. Johnson, Meredith, ill. II. Title.
III. Series: Meiners, Cheri J., 1957– . Learning to get along.
    BF723.F4M45 2003
    152.4'6—dc21
                                                                                                2003010142
ISBN: 978-1-57542-138-4

Reading Level Grade 1; Interest Level Ages 4–8; Fountas & Pinnell Guided Reading Level H

Cover and interior design by Marieka Heinlen
Edited by Marjorie Lisovskis

20 19 18 17 16 15 14 13 12
Printed in China
R18860715

Free Spirit Publishing Inc.
217 Fifth Avenue North, Suite 200
Minneapolis, MN 55401-1299
(612) 338-2068
help4kids@freespirit.com
www.freespirit.com

Free Spirit offers competitive pricing.

Contact edsales@freespirit.com for pricing information on multiple quantity purchases.

Dedication

To my precious daughter Julia
and to each child
who has ever
felt afraid

Acknowledgments

I wish to thank Judy Galbraith and all those at Free Spirit who have enthusiastically supported this book of hope. I especially thank Marieka Heinlen for the lovely design and Margie Lisovskis who, as editor, has shared her wonderful expertise with patience and sensitivity. I am also grateful to Meredith Johnson, whose artistry brings the message to life.

Sometimes I think about things
that could happen.

I might imagine things that frighten me,

like something in the dark
or in my dreams.

Or I might see things that are pretend,
like a spooky movie.

Sometimes scary things are real.

There might be fighting somewhere,
or people who want to hurt other people.

When I think about these things,
I may feel sad, or angry, or afraid.

I'm sorry that bad things happen.

When I don't know what to do,
I can talk to someone who cares about me.

I might talk to my dad or mom
or someone else in my family.

I might also have a baby-sitter
or a neighbor I can talk to.

I know people I can trust.

They take time with me when I need help.

They listen and answer my questions.

They help me understand what is real and what is imaginary.

They comfort me when I feel afraid.

I feel warm and safe with them.

I also know community helpers I can trust.

nurses and doctors

counselors and
religious leaders

sales clerks and postal workers

police officers, firefighters, and soldiers

bus drivers, librarians, and teachers

They all have special jobs that help people.

When I feel worried or afraid, it helps to talk, laugh, and play with friends, too.

I feel better when I am with them.

There are some things I can't change.

If there is nothing I can do about my worries,

I can think of other things instead.

I can read books, or draw pictures.
I can play outdoors, or take a walk.

I can make things, or play games.
I can sing songs.

All these things remind me of the good people and good things in the world.

I may also have a quiet place where I feel safe.

In my quiet place,
I might tell myself something nice.

I might take some deep breaths.

I might say a prayer.

I might think about
the good things in my life.

I want to be strong.

I want to do things I think are right,
even if they seem hard.

When I feel afraid,
I know ways to help myself feel safe.

And I know people I can trust to help me.

Supporting Children When They Feel Afraid

Young children may fear the dark, thunder, spiders, monsters. They may become scared after seeing characters, creatures, or events on TV. They may be afraid of disasters like earthquakes, wildfires, or floods, or of violence they have experienced, seen, or heard of. *When I Feel Afraid* is meant to be a tool parents, teachers, and other adults can use to reassure young children and give them a realistic sense of control concerning their fears. Through sharing the book with adults in their lives, children can come to know that fear is a natural human response, that there are ways to cope with fears, and that there are people who can help them do this.

You may also find the following suggestions helpful. Like the ideas presented in the children's text, these emphasize three key concepts for supporting children—*communicate, clarify,* and *comfort*—along with activities that can help to both soothe and empower children.

Listen and ask questions. Children feel validated when they know someone cares about their fears. By listening carefully and not minimizing their concerns, you show children they can trust you to respect their sensitive feelings. When a child shows or expresses fear, ask questions to invite discussion: "What are you afraid of?" "What are you worried could happen?" "What do you know about?..." "You seem a little worried. Can you tell me about it?" Listen carefully to the child's responses. This approach helps you find out what your child already knows and what his or her specific concerns are.

Talk simply and honestly. Give answers to children according to their age, level of understanding, and interest. Avoid burdening or confusing them with too many details. At the same time, tell the truth with as much kindness as possible. Do not promise outcomes that you can't control; rather, let children know that you and others are doing everything possible to help keep them and their loved ones safe: "I know you're afraid a tornado might come. No one knows exactly where a tornado might go. We can all stay safe in the basement, though." "It's true that being a police officer can be dangerous sometimes. Daddy gets special training, and he does lots of things to stay safe. So I don't worry about him when he's at work."

Use a quiet, calm voice. If a child asks you about your feelings, be gentle and careful as you express your concerns, and as positive as you realistically can: "It's very scary when people get killed. The fighting is far away, though, and we're safe here at school." Children will take their cues from you. If you speak loudly or sound panicky, children will pick up on your intensity. If your voice is steady and you seem composed, children will feel reassured. If you express a hopeful outlook or suggest a way to help, children will see that it's possible to take positive action when bad things happen: "I'm sorry the children's mommy died, too. Our family is safe here at home, though. There's a bank that's collecting money for the children. Maybe we could give some money to help."

Remember, too, that children often tune in to grown-ups' conversations. Whenever possible, discuss adult topics out of children's hearing range.

Clear up confusions. While adults distinguish past events from current ones and the real from the imaginary, children often do not. This is especially true with television. Straighten out facts that have been misunderstood, such as confusing a TV news report with a fictional program. For fears that stem from imagination or confusion, help your child imagine a more positive outcome: "Monsters seem real on TV, but they're make-believe. Let's make up our own monster and draw a picture of it. Maybe it could be a silly one."

Put fears in perspective. Let children know if they are not in danger, or if you consider the danger minimal. If there is a real threat to their safety, answer questions in the most reassuring way that acknowledges both the fear and your efforts to keep children safe: "Car accidents happen sometimes. But I don't think we'll die in a car crash. I drive carefully, and we all wear our seatbelts. Being careful like this helps us be safe."

Sometimes a child will imagine that she or he caused a divorce, an accident, or someone's illness. In these situations, assure children they are not the cause of the bad things happening. Also, allay their fears about what else is likely to happen: "I'm not divorcing *you;* you'll still be in my life."

Read and discuss books that deal with fears. Besides reassuring a child of your caring and concern, books offer a tool to frame a discussion of specific or general fears. They can also help you direct children toward activities that will lift their spirits.

Help children focus on the positive. Children are often more sensitive to events than adults are. While fear can help keep a child safe, it may also show caring and a concern for what happens to oneself or others. Encourage children to use this sensitivity to think of things to do for others; this will bring comfort as children focus on things over which they have control: "I know you're worried that your teacher is sick. I bet he'd be glad to know you're thinking about him. Would you like to draw a get-well picture to send him?"

Also help children see and appreciate what's good in their own lives. One way to do this is by having children make an "I Am Grateful" book. They can make individual books about things they're thankful for, or make a family or class book with pages for each person. When a child feels afraid, share the book as a reminder that the good in life can outweigh the bad.

Be available. Children can become afraid at any time, even while doing something seemingly unrelated to the fear. They may fear something they anticipate happening, something that is happening currently or is being imagined, or something frightening that they remember. At times like these, your mere presence, along with the knowledge that you are available, can be comforting to children.

Tell children that you care about them. More than anything else, children want to know that they are loved and that adults will protect them. Your relationship with them is the most powerful tool they have to help them feel secure. At home, children need to hear, "I love you." Away from home, they need caregivers and teachers to say, "I care what happens to you." Children need all the adults who are responsible for their well-being to tell them, "I'll take care of you." Physical comfort is important, too. Hugs, kisses, pats on the back, shoulder rubs, and even mild rough-and-tumble play reassure children of your affection and concern.

Let children know they are never alone. Children have a fear of being separated from loved ones in a time of crisis, and at other times, too. Assure them that you are leaving them in good hands; let them know when you'll return. Make certain children know who is responsible for their care at a given time—a parent, teacher, childcare provider, or baby-sitter, for example. Also explain the role of various community helpers who are there to keep people safe. Ask children where they might turn for help at the store, at school, or in another child's home. Discuss their ideas, making sure they know how to get help in different settings. Role playing about helpers can support this message.

Keep the lines of communication open between home and school. Parents can alert teachers and caregivers to situations that might affect a child's learning or school interactions. Teachers can let parents know about school experiences so that these can be appropriately discussed and reinforced at home.

Follow a healthy routine. Make sure children (and you) get plenty of sleep, fresh air, and exercise, as well as a balanced diet. This will help provide emotional as well as physical balance. Activities like eating regular meals, having routine playtimes, practicing a sport or musical instrument, and helping with chores build self-esteem and help children feel they have a place in the family or classroom. Carefully planned, predictable transitions from one activity to the next also give a reassuring rhythm to a child's day. Rituals, too, are comforting to a child. This is especially true at night when fears can be greatest. Reading a story, talking about the day, saying prayers, or singing a song are activities that allow a child to relax and rest peacefully.

As part of the home routine, set aside one time each week, perhaps in the evening, specifically for being together as a family. Children feel secure knowing they have regular times with the family to play games, plan activities and outings, and discuss concerns and ideas that interest them. Maintain spiritual traditions as well. Many aspects of religious life can comfort and support children, both with developmental fears and in times of crisis. The familiarity of attending services, seeing friends, and listening and talking to religious leaders can add another dimension of security and stability.

Monitor TV and games. Be aware of what (and how much) children are watching on television. Also be aware of the kinds of video and computer games children play. Young children who see or hear graphic violence, whether it's on the news or part of other programming, can become very fearful. Vivid, violent games can have a similar effect. Controlling children's viewing and gaming activities not only reduces the amount of violence they are likely to see, but also allows time for other worthwhile activities. In addition, family talks about what's happening on TV—what everyone thinks and how they feel watching it—can be a good way to clear up questions and allay fears.

Encourage healthy play. Let children draw pictures as a way to release and express their emotions. Writing stories and other creative play are also useful problem-solving tools. Do not allow play in which children purposely hurt or try to hurt others; redirect children to cooperative ways to play instead.

Prepare for changes and emergencies. Prepare children for new situations that may be stressful. Discuss expectations and give reassurance before events such as starting school, making a switch to a new classroom, moving, or experiencing a family change like a divorce, a marriage, or a baby's arrival. Also develop a family plan for various emergencies that could affect children. Talk together about safety measures such as how and when to dial 911, where everyone can meet when community sirens sound, and what to do for fire safety. Make sure children know their address as well as phone numbers where family adults can be reached. Children can also help in finding and assembling items for a family emergency kit. You'll find details about this at *www.redcross.org.* Click on "Prepare Your Home and Family."

Help children reach out to others. They might write to someone who is sick or to public servants like firefighters. They can write to leaders and politicians to let their voices be heard. Children also love to draw pictures, write stories or poems, make crafts and small gifts, and help with chores. Help your child think of people who may appreciate their letters and gifts such as friends, family, relatives, and those in institutional settings like hospitals or nursing homes. Encourage children to donate items such as gently used toys, clothing, or books to people who are in need. The Red Cross accepts money for relief aid; local charities accept donations of clothing and furniture. Toiletries and canned goods are welcome at shelters and community kitchens. Children can also participate in walkathons that raise money to fight diseases.

Teach children to appreciate differences. People have different physical traits and abilities, interests, customs, and beliefs. Show through teaching and example that the different ways people look, talk, act, and learn are valuable and interesting. Help children respect and appreciate all kinds of diversity; foster their curiosity about others and encourage them to share their own unique traits and experiences as well. This helps children learn not to fear the unknown and supports understanding of people from different backgrounds.

If needed, seek outside help. Despite all your efforts, behavioral changes that affect eating, sleep, or play may occur when children are afraid or aware of a crisis. Some temporary allowances in behavior, as well as extra time with you, may give an added measure of comfort. If a fear is limiting or overtaking a child's everyday life, though, seek professional help. You might ask a pediatrician, guidance counselor, psychologist, or social worker to recommend a counselor or child development specialist. Let the agency or counselor know if cost is a concern; ask if services can be covered by a medical plan or whether low-cost or free assistance is available.

Additional Resources for Supporting Children

The following resources offer support for dealing with young children's fears. For books about specific fears, check with your library or bookstore.

APA American Psychological Association Help Center
www.apa.org/helpcenter/index.aspx • Provides recommendations for fostering young children's resilience during times of social upheaval.

"Children and Fear of War and Terrorism: Tips for Parents and Teachers"
www.nasponline.org/resources/crisis_safety/children_war_general.aspx • Information and guidance from the National Association of School Psychologists.

"Mommy, I'm Scared": How TV and Movies Frighten Children and What We Can Do to Protect Them
by Joanne Cantor, Ph.D. (New York: Harcourt, 1998). Presents research, case studies, and theories of developmental psychology to illustrate effects of media violence, along with strategies to help children cope with media-induced fears.

PBS Parents
www.pbs.org/parents/child-development • A site with informative articles on a range of early childhood development topics.

Sesame Workshop
www.sesameworkshop.org • Search for the You Can Ask project to find video and print content for parents and caregivers to help children handle stress and fear.

There's a Big, Beautiful World Out There!
by Nancy Carlson (New York: Puffin Books, 2004). A children's book that fosters courage, overcoming anxieties, and a positive outlook.

Free Spirit's **Learning to Get Along®** Series

Help children learn, understand, and practice basic social and emotional skills. Real-life situations, diversity, and concrete examples make these read-aloud books appropriate for childcare settings, schools, and the home. *Each book: 40 pp., color illust., PB, 9" x 9", ages 4–8.*

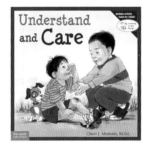

Learning to Get Along® bilingual editions

Each book: 48 pp., color illust., PB, 9" x 9", ages 4–8.

www.freespirit.com | 800.735.7323 | Volume discounts: edsales@freespirit.com | Speakers bureau: speakers@freespirit.com